Michael

Bostic

coughlin

I SPY
FUN HOUSE

A BOOK OF
PICTURE
RIDDLES

Photographs by Walter Wick

Riddles by Jean Marzollo

Cartwheel B·O·O·K·S·®

SCHOLASTIC INC.

New York   Toronto   London   Auckland   Sydney
Mexico City   New Delhi   Hong Kong   Buenos Aires

For my sister, Jenny

W. W.

For Danny, David, and Claudio

J.M.

Also available in bookstores:

I SPY: A BOOK OF PICTURE RIDDLES

I SPY CHRISTMAS

I SPY MYSTERY

Book design by Carol Devine Carson

Text copyright © 1993 by Jean Marzollo.
Photographs copyright © 1993 by Walter Wick.
All rights reserved. Published by Scholastic Inc.

CARTWHEEL BOOKS is a registered trademark of Scholastic Inc.

Library of Congress Cataloging-in-Publication Data

Wick, Walter.
  I spy: funhouse / photographs by Walter Wick; riddles by Jean
Marzollo; designed by Carol Devine Carson.
    p.   cm.
  Summary: Rhyming verses ask readers to find hidden objects in the
photographs.
  ISBN 0-590-46293-8
  1. Picture puzzles — Juvenile literature.   [1. Picture puzzles.]
I. Marzollo, Jean.   II. Title.
GV1507.P47W523   1993
793.3 — dc20   92-16425
                                                          CIP
                                                          AC

40 39 38 37 36 35   05 06 07
                       Printed in Mexico   49

First Scholastic printing, March 1993

TABLE OF CONTENTS

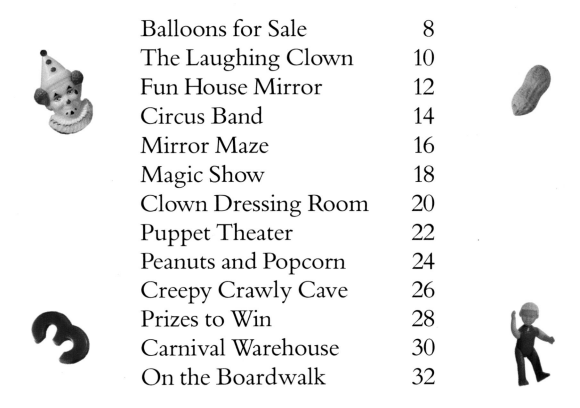

fun house (*n*): a building in an amusement park that contains various devices designed to startle or amuse

Picture riddles fill this book;
Turn the pages! Take a look!

Amuse your mind, startle your eye;
Read the rhymes and play I Spy!

I spy a fan and five white boats,
Antlers, a kite, and a whale that floats;

A seagull, a boot, two owlish eyes,
A little red pail, and eight butterflies.

I spy an apple, a polka-dot Y,
A quail, a shovel, a man with a tie;

Two whistles, a trumpet, a cowbell, a clock,
A banjo, a racket, and DOT on a block.

I spy a clothespin, a horse with no rider,
Scissors, a whistle, a traveling spider;

A cherry on a cone, a red and yellow BOX—
Now turn upside down, and find a red fox.

I spy a banjo, a bird on the wing,
An old bottle cap, a crown for a king;

A button, a B, a fish from the sea,
Three thimbles, a lock, and a DO RE MI.

I spy a penguin, a clown with a seal,
A butterfly, giraffe, a toy ferris wheel;

Three hanging red swords, an ostrich, a duck—
Go through the doors if you run out of luck.

I spy a shoe, a diamond jack,
A magic coin, a blue thumbtack;

A spoon, a door, a plane, a bat,
A soccer ball, and a card-trick CAT.

I spy a fish, five clothespins, a rose,
The reflection of an elephant's nose;

A baby bottle, a small bobby pin,
A sword, a monkey, and O's place to win.

I spy a key, an eye patch, a bell,
A match, a swan, a phone, and a shell;

Three red hearts, a watering can,
Ten dominoes, and a mushroom man.

I spy a lobster, a small circus flag,
A racket, a skateboard, a horse shopping bag;

Half of a melon, the stem of a pear,
A button, a basket, a boat, and a bear.

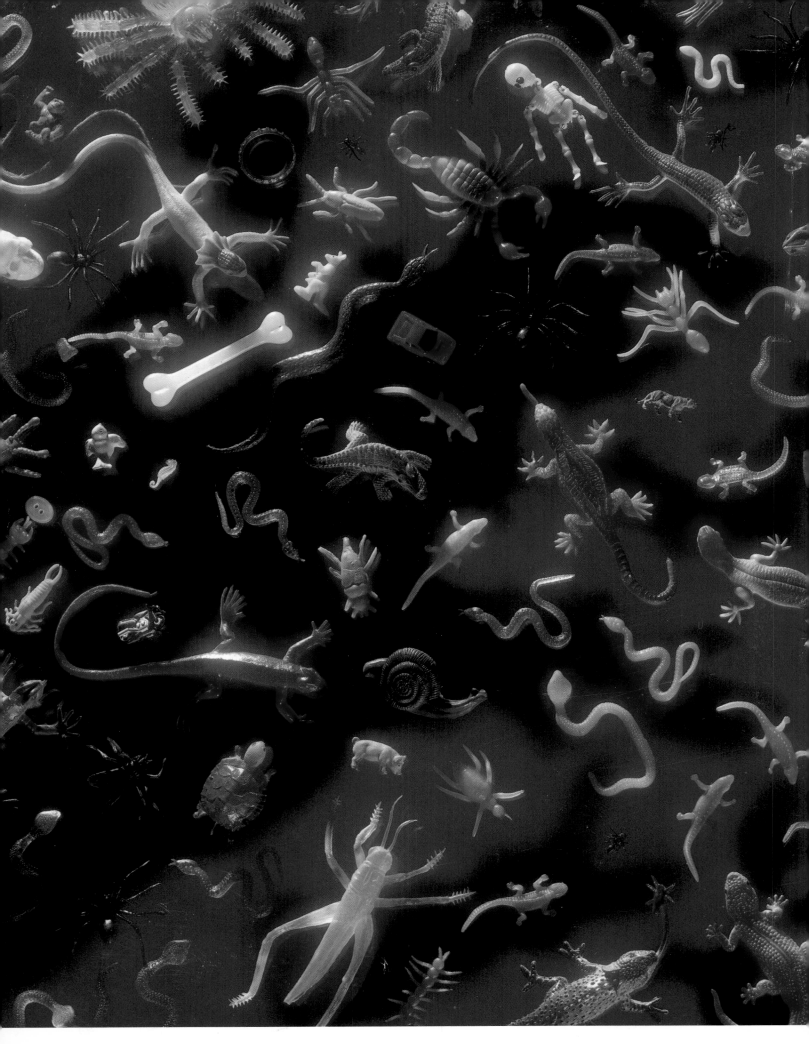

I spy an eyeball, a baby kangaroo,
Seven black ants, and a bird that's blue;

A turtle, a sea horse, a shark, and a snail,
A piece of twine, and a very weird nail.

I spy a fire truck, an anklet of LOVE,
A six, three balloons, a bear's baseball glove;

One green dragonfly, six orange bills,
A straw hat, a G, a skateboard, and THRILLS.

I spy a ladder, two green mice,
A clown with pliers, three little dice;

A spider, a panther, a gumball machine,
A nosey bee, and a curvy queen.

I spy WONDER, a man with a cane,
Three safety pins, and an old-fashioned plane;

A girl jumping rope, a thumbtack, a spoon,
A man with a mop, and the man in the moon.

EXTRA CREDIT RIDDLES

"Find Me" Riddle

My ears are rather long and funny;

I'm in every picture; I am a _____

Find the Pictures That Go with These Riddles:

I spy a whistle, a little guitar,

A snake, a key, and a shiny star.

I spy a plane, a round bottle cap,

Bananas, a three, and a little mousetrap.

I spy a baseball, a bat, and a mouse,

A bone, panda's nose, and a backwards HOUSE.

I spy a moustache, a popped piece of corn,

An unshelled peanut, and a shy unicorn.

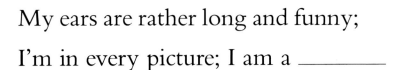

I spy a gear and a bumblebee,

Two red flags, and a green palm tree.

I spy a squirrel, a watermelon slice,
A tiger's tail, and a pair of dice.

I spy two large clown puzzle faces,
Two calves, and a fire truck in seventeen places.

I spy a trumpet, a chair, and a G,
A magnet, two bikes, and a man on his knee.

I spy a bell, a flashlight, a train,
A shoe for your keys, and a loose candy chain.

I spy blue glitter about to fall,
A pan, a snake, and a seal with a ball.

I spy a pail, a lace for a shoe,
A phone, a bone, and a tiny two.

I spy a stork, a baseball, a car,
A fireman's hat, and a yellow star.

I spy a horseshoe, a drum, a kazoo,
And all of the letters for PINK in blue.

Write Your Own Picture Riddles

There are many more hidden objects and many more possibilities for riddles in this book. Write some rhyming picture riddles yourself, and try them out with friends.

Special Acknowledgments

We are very pleased to acknowledge the many people at Scholastic who have helped with the *I SPY* books, particularly Grace Maccarone, senior editor; Bernette Ford, editorial director of Cartwheel Books; Jean Feiwel, associate publisher; Barbara Marcus, publisher; as well as Edie Weinberg, John Illingworth, John Mason, Doris Bass, Lenora Todaro, Cathy Lusk, Heidi Sachner, Michelle Lewy, Jill O'Brien, Arlene Chernenko, Alan Barnes, Mary Marotta, Nancy Smith, John Simko, and Linda Savio.

We'd like to thank Linda Cheverton-Wick for artistic insight and research help on the fun house theme, and Molly Friedrich of The Aaron M. Priest Literary Agency for wise and constructive guidance.

We are grateful to photo assistant Kathy O'Donnell for her tireless attention to detail; Bruce Morozko for codesigning and constructing the sets for "The Laughing Clown" and "Puppet Show," magician Larry Bramble for his "Magic Show" props, and Frank and Ray Hills for letting us use their collection of miniature circus figures. And finally, we would like to pay special tribute to the world of fairs, circuses, and carnivals, whose unique visual qualities and spirit of fun inspired this book.

Walter Wick and Jean Marzollo

How the Pictures in This Book Were Made

Except for "The Laughing Clown" and "Puppet Show," which were codesigned and constructed by Bruce Morozko, all the sets for the pictures in this book were created by photographer Walter Wick. The sets, approximately 4′ by 8′ each, were made of wood, fabric, toys, props, circus paraphernalia, and mirrors.

As each set for *Fun House* was constructed, Walter Wick and Jean Marzollo conferred on the various objects in the sets, selecting them for their rhyming potential, as well as their aesthetic and playful qualities. The objects were hidden so they would be fun for readers to find. Wick lit each set carefully to create the right shadows, depth, and fun house mood. Finally, he photographed the set with an 8″ by 10″ view camera. Each set was then dismantled before the next one was created. They survive only as photographs to inspire rhyming, riddle making, visual creativity, and the exciting challenge of the *I Spy* hunt.

Walter Wick, the inventor of many photographic games for *Games* magazine, is the photographer of the immensely popular *I Spy: A Book of Picture Riddles* and *I Spy Christmas*. He is also a free-lance photographer for Scholastic's *Let's Find Out* and *Super Science*. His credits include over 300 magazine and book covers, including *Newsweek, Fortune,* and *Psychology Today*. This is his third book for Scholastic.

Jean Marzollo has written many rhyming children's books, including *I Spy: A Book of Picture Riddles, I Spy Christmas, Halloween Cats, In 1492, Pretend You're a Cat, The Rebus Treasury, The Teddy Bear Book,* and *Close Your Eyes*. She is also the author of fiction for beginning readers, such as *Cannonball Chris, Soccer Sam, The Green Ghost of Appleville,* and *The Baby Unicorn,* as well as nonfiction books, such as *The Helping Hands Handbook*. **Carol Devine Carson**, the book designer for all the *I Spy* books, is art director for a major publishing house in New York City. She is also the illustrator and designer of *The Rebus Treasury*. For over fifteen years, Marzollo and Carson together produced Scholastic's kindergarten magazine, *Let's Find Out*.